Eating

By Paul Bennett

Belitha Press

612-3

First published in Great Britain in 1997 by
Belitha Press Limited
London House, Great Eastern Wharf
Parkgate Road, London SW11 4NQ

Reprinted 1998

Editor: Veronica Ross
Series designer: Hayley Cove
Photographer: Claire Paxton
Illustrator: Cilla Eurich
Picture researcher: Diana Morris
Consultant: Elizabeth Atkinson

ISBN 1 85561 594 0 (hardback)
ISBN 1 85561 778 1 (paperback)

Printed in Hong Kong

Photo credits
Axiom/Jim Holmes: 27t.
Zefa/Stockmarket/Craig Tuttle: 17t.

Thanks to models Meera, Jodie, Sam,
Topel, Ricky

Words in **bold** are explained in the list
of useful words on pages 30 and 31.

Contents

Why do I need to eat?

Food keeps you alive. You need to eat in order to stay **healthy** and to feel fit and well.

The useful parts of food, called **nutrients**, are used to help your body grow and **repair** itself.

Food is body fuel. It gives you **energy** for playing and working. Your body uses energy all the time.

It is important to eat three meals every day to stay healthy and feeling good.

A balanced diet

There are lots of different types of food. Fruit, meat, vegetables, bread and cheese are just a few.

Can you think of any more?

What are your favourite foods?

The food
you eat every
day is called your
diet. A balanced diet
is one that has all
the nutrients your
body needs.

Different foods
have different nutrients in
them. To stay healthy, you
need to eat different types
of food so that you get all
the nutrients you need.

Body-building foods

Body-building foods are rich in **proteins**. Proteins build your **muscles**, skin, **bones**, and all the other parts of your body.

Proteins help you to grow. They also help your body to repair itself.

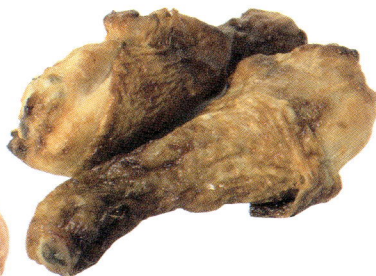

Proteins are
found in lots
of different foods, such
as meat, fish, eggs, milk,
cheese, nuts and beans.

It is important
to eat some
of these foods
every day.

Energy foods

You use up lots of energy when you are running around. Energy comes from foods that are rich in **carbohydrates**.

Carbohydrates are found in potatoes, rice, pasta, bread and fruit.

You need lots of these foods if you are exercising or playing games.

Sweet foods, such as cakes and chocolate, are full of carbohydrates too. But too many cakes and chocolate can make you unhealthy.

Fatty foods

You only need a small amount of fat in your diet to stay healthy.

Fats are found in foods such as butter, cheese, chocolate and biscuits.

Avocados, vegetable oils, sardines and meat also contain lots of fat.

Many people try to cut down the amount of fat in their diet. They grill food instead of frying it, and they use skimmed milk (milk without the cream).

If you eat too many fatty foods, such as these fried **samosas**, you may become overweight.

Fats give you lots of energy.

Vitamins and minerals

A balanced diet will give you all the **vitamins** and **minerals** you need.

There are many different kinds of vitamins. They keep your body working properly.

Vitamin C is found in vegetables and fruit. It helps cuts to heal, and helps you to fight off colds and flu.

Vitamins and minerals are found in many different foods. Fish, oranges and tomatoes contain vitamins.

Milk, cheese and green vegetables are good sources of minerals.

Calcium is a mineral found in milk. It helps to keep your bones and teeth healthy and strong.

All about fibre

Fibre is an important part of a balanced diet. It contains no goodness, but it helps you to **digest** the food that you eat.

Fibre also helps to fill you up.

Fibre is found in plants like the wheat shown here. Wholemeal flour is made from wheat. It is used to make bread.

Foods that are rich in fibre include **wholemeal bread**, fruit and vegetables with the skins left on, lentils and beans.

17

Water for life

You would not live long without water. All the parts of your body need water, so you must have plenty of drinks to stay fit and healthy.

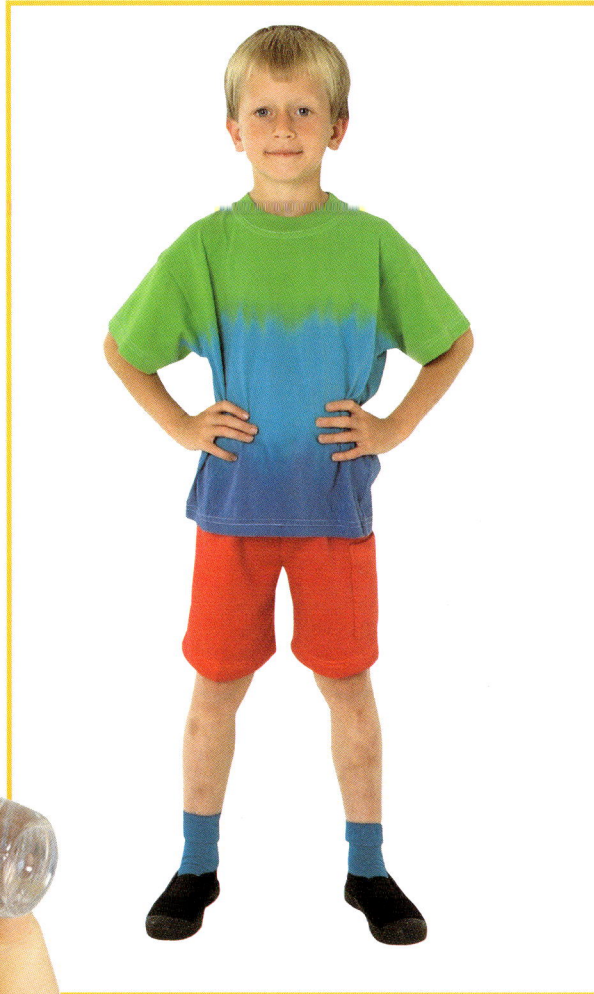

When you are thirsty, your mouth feels dry. This is your body's way of telling you to drink some water.

Your body is about two-thirds water. Does it look like this?

You lose water when you **sweat** and when you go to the toilet. You also lose water when you breathe out.

It's important to replace the water your body loses.

Vegetables and fruit contain a lot of water. Coconut milk is almost all water.

Chewing and swallowing

When you eat, your teeth break the food into tiny pieces. The food is mixed with your **saliva**, and turns into mushy lumps.

front tooth   **back tooth**

Your front teeth are used for biting.

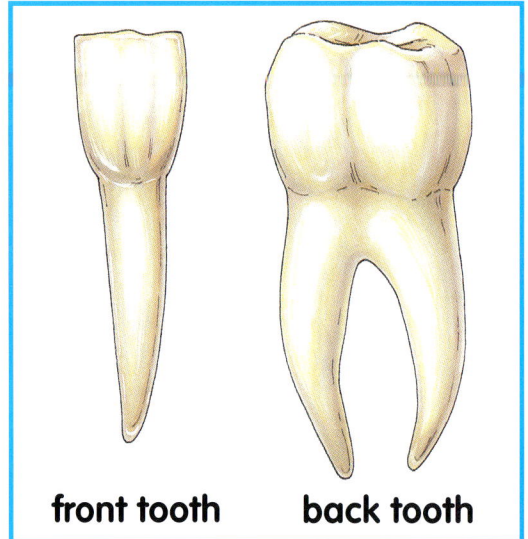

Your back teeth are used for chewing.

Your body breaks down the food and takes the goodness from it. This is called digestion.

When you swallow, the food goes down a tube into your stomach.

chewed food

food tube

The food stays in your stomach before passing into a long and tightly-folded tube called the intestine.

stomach

intestine

Food that cannot be digested comes out of your body when you go to the toilet.

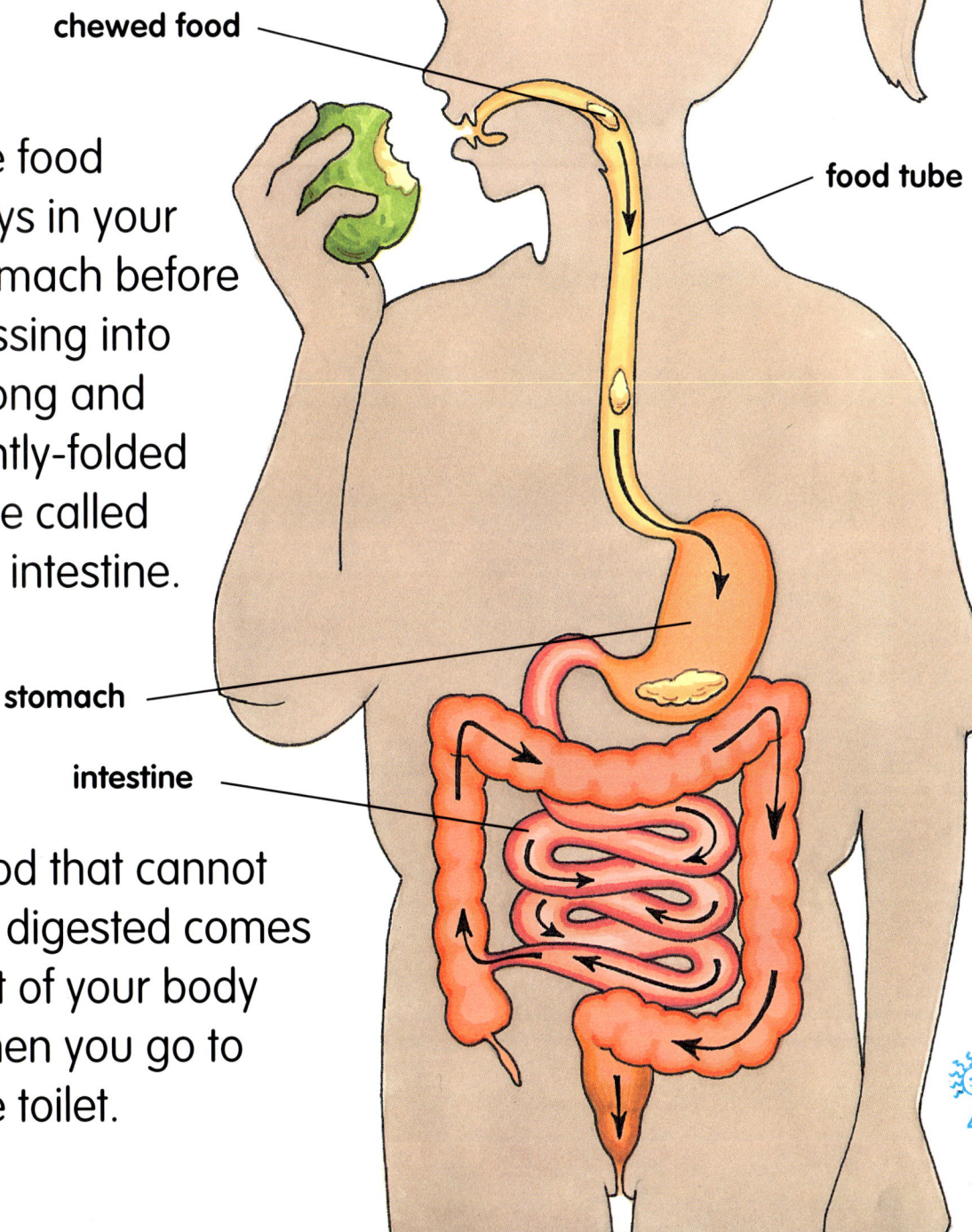

21

Digesting your food

Inside your stomach, the food is squeezed by your stomach walls and mixed with special **juices**, until it is very soft and mushy.

Sometimes your stomach makes funny gurgling noises as your food is being digested.

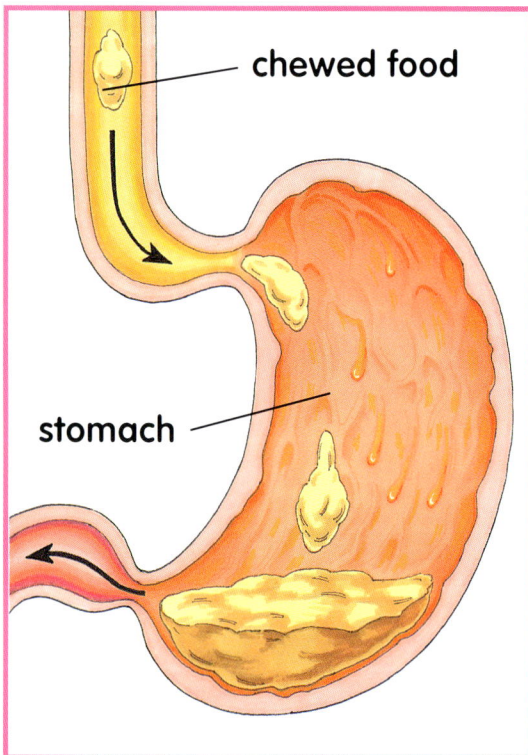

chewed food

stomach

A main meal stays in your stomach for more than three hours. A simple meal stays for much less time.

The mushy food passes out of your stomach and into your intestine.

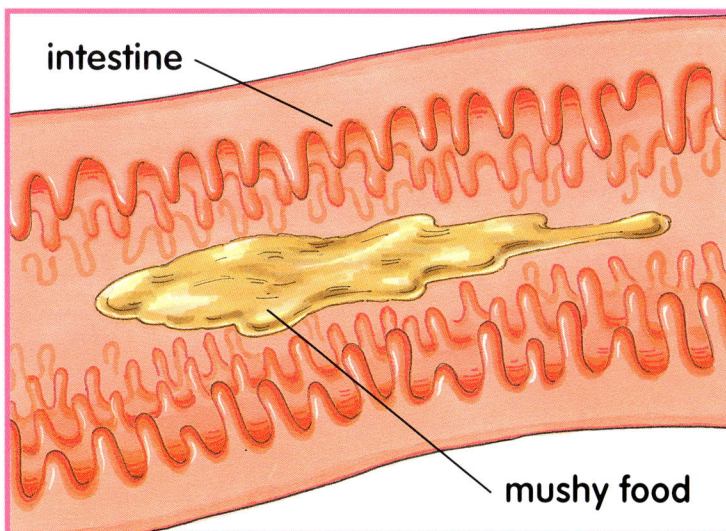

intestine

mushy food

Nutrients in the food pass through the walls of the intestine into your bloodstream. Your **blood** carries the nutrients to every part of your body.

The whole process of digestion takes between 10 and 20 hours.

23

Snacks and junk food

If you ate only chocolate, biscuits and crisps and drank only fizzy drinks, you would soon become unhealthy.

Food that has no goodness left in it is called junk food. Some **take-away food** is junk food.

Too many sweet things can make your teeth **decay**.

A sandwich made with
wholemeal bread,
and an apple or pear
is a healthy snack for
lunchtime.

If you feel hungry
between meals, eat
a piece of fruit or
some nuts instead
of a chocolate bar.

Fruit juice
is better for
you than fizzy drinks.

Special food

We need food to live, but we also use it to celebrate birthdays, weddings and religious festivals.

These people are at a Hindu wedding feast. The food has been given by the bride's family.

Vegetarians are people who do not eat meat. They may believe it is wrong to eat animals.

Some people are **allergic** to such foods as strawberries, chocolate and nuts. If they eat these foods they will become sick.

I ate too much!

It is not good for you to eat too much of anything in one go. You will get stomachache and may even be sick!

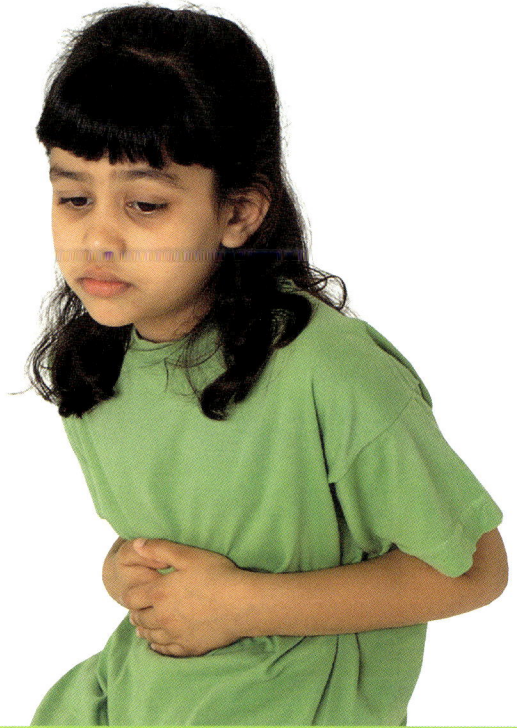

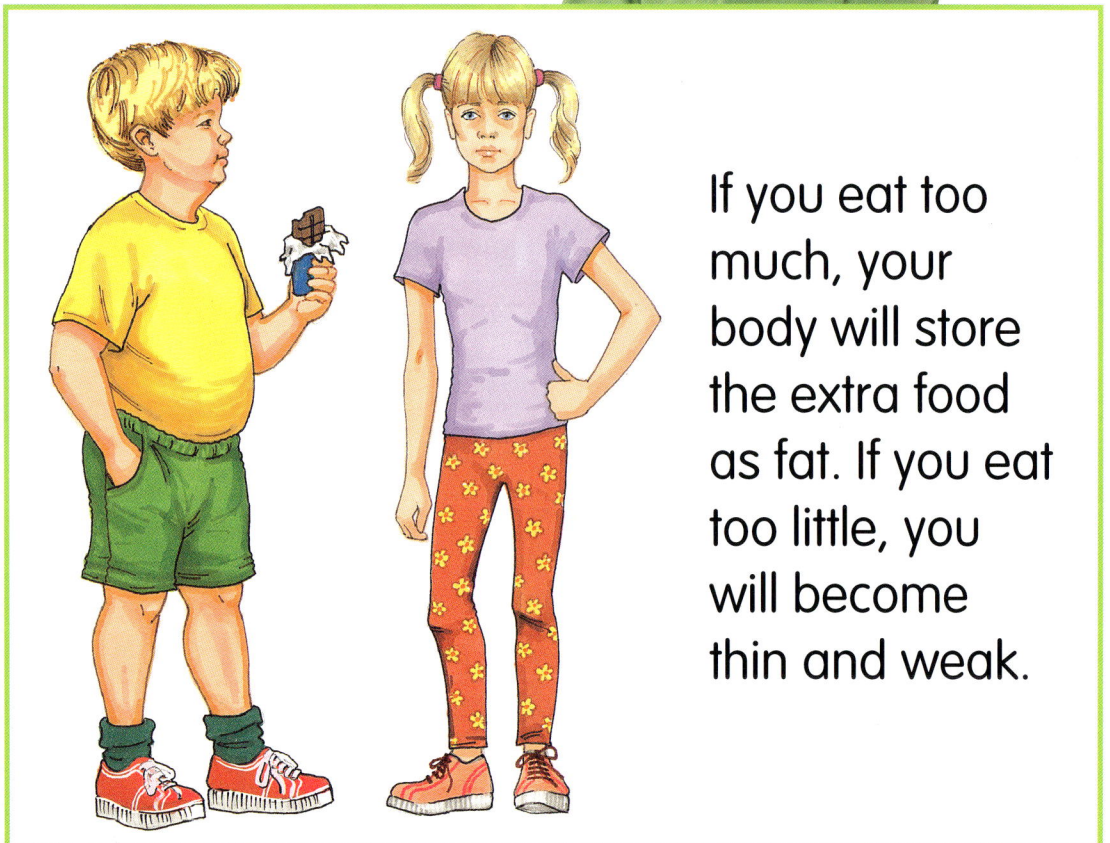

If you eat too much, your body will store the extra food as fat. If you eat too little, you will become thin and weak.

Foods that contain a lot
of fat and carbohydrates,
like pizza, cakes and
burgers, taste nice
but don't eat them
too often!

You will know if you
are eating the right
amount for you if
you are fit and lively,
and are
neither too
thin nor
too fat.

Useful words

Allergic
To be sensitive to something. This might be a food which makes you feel ill.

Blood
The red liquid that is pumped around your body by your heart.

Bones
The strong and hard parts inside your body.

Carbohydrates
The part of some foods that give you energy.

Decay
To go bad or to rot.

Digest
To break food up into smaller and smaller parts so that your body can use the nutrients it needs.

Energy
What you need to be able to play and work without feeling tired.

Healthy
Fit and well.

Juices
Liquids in your stomach that help to break down food.

Minerals
Natural substances, such as calcium, that help your body to stay healthy.

Muscles
The soft, stretchy parts inside your body that make you move.

Nutrients
The useful parts of food that your body needs to stay healthy.

Proteins
The part of food which is used by the body for growth and repair.

Repair
To mend.

Saliva
A liquid in the mouth that prepares food for swallowing.

Samosa
A fried pastry snack filled with meat or vegetables.

Sweat
Wetness from the skin.

Take-away food
Cooked food that is bought at a shop or restaurant.

Vitamins
Chemicals found in all sorts of food. Your body must have them to help you grow and stay well.

Wholemeal bread
Bread that is made with the whole wheat grain. White bread is made with only part of the grain.

Index